Simply Science

RAIN & SHINE

Felicia Law & Steve Way

Illustrations: Steve Boulter & Xact Studio

Diagrams: Ralph Pitchford

AUTHORS: FELICIA LAW
STEVE WAY

ILLUSTRATORS:
STEVE BOULTER
XACT STUDIO

MAPS: GEO-INNOVATIONS UK
RALPH PITCHFORD

DESIGN: RALPH PITCHFORD

ISBN 978-1-906292-21-8
Printed in China

PHOTO CREDITS:

p.4–5 Daniel Leclair/CORBIS.
p.6 Nikola Bilic/Shutterstock Inc.
p.8 Pot of Grass Productions/Shutterstock Inc.
p.9 Jim Reed/CORBIS.
p.10 (cl) Jim Reed/SCIENCE PHOTO LIBRARY.,
(c) Andrey Plis/Shutterstock Inc.,
(cr) David Lewis/Shutterstock Inc.
p.11 Lars Christensen/Shutterstock Inc.
p.13 (tl) Jostein Hauge/Shutterstock Inc.,
(r) Bateleur/Shutterstock Inc.
p.14 Jens Mayer/Shutterstock Inc.
p.14–15 Mihaicalin/Shutterstock Inc.
p.15 Mark Bond/Shutterstock Inc.
p.16–17 Jan Martin Will/Shutterstock Inc.
p.17 Bernhard Edmaier/SCIENCE PHOTO LIBRARY.
p.18 Darla Hallmark/Shutterstock Inc.
p.20 Jhaz Photography/Shutterstock Inc.
p.22 (cl) NASA/JPL.,
(tr) NASA/Dryden Flight Research Center.
p.22–23 NASA.
p.24 Jozef Sedmak/Shutterstock Inc.
p.25 Jakob Metzger/Shutterstock Inc.
p.26 (bl) Hugo Maes/Shutterstock Inc.,
(br) Chee-Onn Leong/Shutterstock Inc.
p.27 (tr) Zastavkin/Shutterstock Inc.,
(cr) Olga Shelego/Shutterstock Inc.,
(bl) Hinrich Baesemann/CORBIS,
(br) Pichugin Dmitry/Shutterstock Inc.

Cover
Mihaicalin/Shutterstock Inc.,

Simply Science

RAIN & SHINE

Contents

What is weather?

What's the weather like today? Has the pouring rain meant you couldn't play games out-of-doors? Is it so sunny you need a cool shower? Or so icy cold, you're wearing a double layer of sweaters? You can't get away from the weather - it changes all the time - and forces you to change with it!

Weather describes the **temperature** of a place; how hot or cold it is. Weather describes the air; whether it's **moving** up or down in the atmosphere. It describes the kind of **wind** that's blowing and measures how much **rain** is falling - or not falling.

Weather is all about what is happening in the atmosphere that surrounds our Earth.

Weather can be:

rainy and damp

dry

hot

icy cold

stormy

... or still.

4

Some buildings have to be
built to withstand the worst
weather conditions – like
this lighthouse!

Wind is the movement of air surounding our Earth. There is almost always some wind, even if it's very light. Winds usually begin when air moves from an area of high pressure to one of low pressure.

Measuring the atmospheric pressure

A barometer is an instrument that is used to measure pressure in the atmosphere. An aneroid barometer has a dial marked in units of pressure. A needle moves over the dial as the pressure changes. When the air pressure increases, it pushes down on one or more metal containers.

High and low

Scientists are able to measure the weight of the air that is pressing down on Earth. This measurement is what they call 'atmospheric pressure'. The lower the ground, the more air is pressing down on it. Pressure is higher in a valley and lower on top of a mountain peak.

High pressure is an area of the atmosphere where the atmospheric pressure is high. High pressure areas usually bring clear, dry weather.

Low pressure is an area of the atmosphere where the atmospheric pressure is low. During a period of low pressure, the weather is usually wet.

Windy names

Polar winds are cold winds that blow off the Arctic and Antarctic regions.

Trade winds blow around the Tropics towards the Equator.

Monsoons are winds that change direction with the seasons – summer monsoons are mainly westerly and bring lots of rain. Winter monsoons tend to be easterly and cause drought.

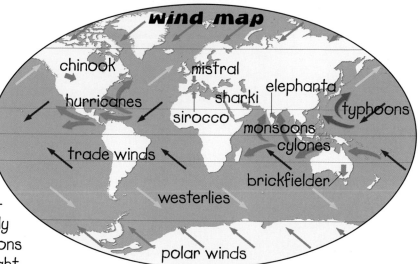

wind map

chinook

mistral

elephanta

hurricanes

sharki

typhoons

sirocco

monsoons

cylones

trade winds

brickfielder

westerlies

polar winds

Many winds have special names:

The **mistral** and **sirocco** blow around Mediterranean countries.

The **brickfielder** is a wind from the desert of Southern Australia.

A **chubasco** is a violent squall with thunder and lightning, that happens during the rainy season along the west coast of Central America.

The **elephanta** is a strong southerly or southeasterly wind which blows on the Malabar coast of India.

Sharki is a southeasterly wind which sometimes blows in the Persian Gulf.

A **willy-willy** is a tropical cyclone off the north-east coast of Australia.

The **chinook** blows down the eastern slopes of the Rocky Mountains of the USA.

Which way?

You can always tell which way the wind is blowing by licking your finger and holding it up. Your finger will feel colder on the part that the wind is blowing on.

Windy weather

The strength of the wind is measured by scientists using the Beaufort scale. This goes from 0 to 12 and measures the effect of the wind on land.

Keep your hat on!

Anemometer and weather vane

An anemometer is an instrument that measures the speed of the wind. The wind turns small cups that are attached to a rod. The harder the wind is blowing, the faster the cups turn. The weather vane shows which direction the wind is blowing.

0	Calm	Smoke rises straight up.
1	Light air	Only the lightest things are stirred.
2	Light breeze	Wind felt on face, leaves rustle.
3	Gentle breeze	Leaves and small twigs in constant motion; light flag will blow out.
4	Moderate breeze	Raises dust and loose paper; small branches are moved.
5	Fresh breeze	Small trees in leaf begin to sway. Good weather for flying kites!
6	Strong breeze	Large branches in motion; whistling heard in telegraph wires.

Wild winds!

A **hurricane** is the strongest kind of wind there is. It blows in a circular pattern. There is an area of calm at the centre - called the eye, and the wind swirls round this. Hurricanes bring heavy rain and thunderstorms.

A **cyclone** is a hurricane that blows in from the Indian or Pacific oceans. A hurricane blowing in from the northern Pacific is known as a **typhoon**. Hurricanes will destroy property and cause flooding near the coast. They can raise the sea level 6 metres above normal.

A tornado

7	Near gale	Whole trees in motion; difficult to walk against the wind.
8	Gale	Breaks twigs off trees; stops your progress.
9	Severe gale	Slight structural damage occurs (roof damage).
10	Storm	Seldom experienced inland; trees uprooted; structural damage occurs.
11	Violent storm	Very rarely experienced; accompanied by wide-spread damage.
12	Hurricane	Very rarely experienced; wide-spread damamge; flooding near the coast.

A **tornado**, or whirlwind or twister, is a kind of small hurricane. The wind spins around an area of calm in the centre. But it spins much faster than in a hurricane, moving over the ground at high speed and destroying everything in its path. Fortunately it spins so fast, it soon loses energy and only lasts for one or two hours.

Dust devils are a type of whirlwind that blow in desert areas. They pick up dust as they move and can travel at speeds of up to 40 kilometres an hour. They usually occur in the afternoon when the land surface heats up rapidly.

The jet stream
High above the Earth, there is a narrow band of very fast-moving winds. This is known as the jet stream.

9

Rainy days

In most parts of the world, water falls from clouds in the sky from time to time. It may not fall every day or even every month, but when it does, it falls as rain or light dew, or, if it's especially cold, as sleet, hail or snow.

Large drops of water fall as in thunderstorms or heavy showers. The smallest waterdrops fall as drizzle. The amount of rain that falls in any place is called its rainfall.

Hailstones form in huge storm clouds. They can be as big as tennis balls when they fall, causing a lot of damage.

Dew forms at night when the temperature drops. The droplets condense and then fall onto the ground or onto plants.

Measuring the wetness in the air

Humid is the word used to describe the atmosphere when it contains lots of water vapour. Warm air holds more water vapour than cold air, so really damp and humid air is mostly found in the hot steamy jungles and rainforests near the Equator.

Hygrometer

A hygrometer is an instrument that measures how much humidity there is in the air. There are different kinds. A mechanical hygrometer uses human hair – always blond hair – attached to a dial. The hair expands or contracts depending on the humidity.

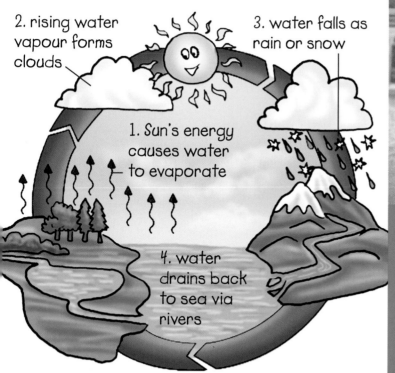

2. rising water vapour forms clouds

3. water falls as rain or snow

1. Sun's energy causes water to evaporate

4. water drains back to sea via rivers

Water vapour in the air gets colder and heavier as it rises and changes back into liquid, forming clouds. This process is known as condensation.

A **cloudburst** is a sudden shower of heavy rain. These often happen in periods of warm and stormy weather.

A **hygroscope** is an instrument that shows any changes in the humidity level. A strip of seaweed is a good hygroscope because it becomes soft and bendy when the weather is humid, and hard and dry when it isn't.

Acid rain

Acid rain falls from clouds that have become full of unwanted chemicals in the atmosphere. Acid rain may fall near cities where factories gush poisonous fumes, such as sulphur dioxide and nitric acid, into the air. Or they are carried on the wind far from the factories. Nitric acid forms as the fumes mix with the water in the clouds. This acid rain poisons the soil it falls on and the rivers it flows into.
It kills trees and animals and makes people feel unwell.

Weather forecasting

You can see what the weather's like today, but who's going to tell you what it will be like tomorrow – or the next day, or the day after that? This is called weather forecasting.

The real name for weather forecasting is meteorology. You can see meteorologists everyday on the TV, pointing at a large map and telling you where the rain will fall or where high winds will blow. You probably think it looks easy, or even – that they might be guessing!

But meteorologists are very skilled scientists. They have to watch what is happening all over the globe, not just the part where they live, because weather is a moving thing.

They measure the wind, the temperature and the atmospheric pressure to predict how the weather will change from place to place over the next few days.

Weather speak

Words a meteorologist must understand:

An anticyclone decribes a high pressure zone surrounded by winds circulating in the opposite direction to a cyclone.

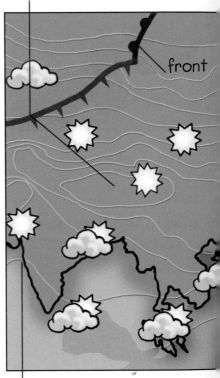

front

Isobar is a line on a weather map that shows places that have the same atmospheric pressure. If the points are close together, it's windy.

A front describes a sharp change in the temperature of the air. A front happens when a mass of cold air meets a mass of warm air. A cold front is the edge of a cold mass of air, and a warm front lies at the edge of a warm mass of air.

Cyclone – A weather system with low pressure at its centre around which winds are blowing.

Depression – An area of low pressure bringing rain, cloud and wind.

I don't know! I'm just the weatherman!

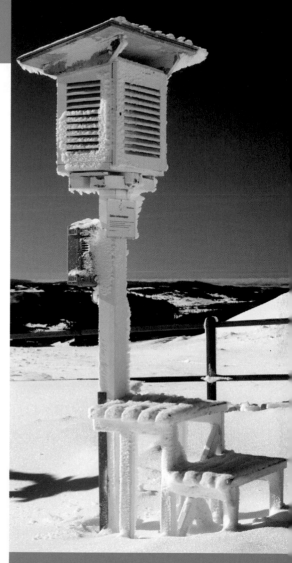

Weather stations

Weather stations have been set up around the world to help meteorologists to predict the weather and see if it has changed over time. This weather station contains special instruments to measure the weather.

A cold day

If you live in a part of the world where your fingers tingle with cold on a cold day, you will know about wintry weather.

A hoar frost is made of crystals of ice.

Frost occurs when the air or ground temperature is so cold that ice forms. Moisture in the air, called water vapour, condenses and then freezes on the soil and plants.

Hail is frozen raindrops. The pieces of ice in hail are called hailstones. They can be as large as 5 centimetres across.

Sleet is a mixture of rain and snow. It can be snow or hail which has half-melted as it fell from the clouds.

Snow is water that forms in the clouds as crystals of ice. This can only happen when it is so cold that the water vapour in the clouds freezes.

A **blizzard** is a fierce snowstorm. These are common in icy regions such as the open wastes of the Arctic and Antarctica.

Ice is frozen water. Water freezes at 0 degrees Celsius or 32 degrees Fahrenheit. Salty water freezes at a lower temperature, so although the water in a large lake will freeze, the water in the sea does not. When water becomes ice, it swells up and takes more space. Even so, ice is still lighter and less dense than water, which is why it floats on the surface.

I'm freezing!

Temperature

Fahrenheit is one of the scales used for measuring temperature. On the Fahrenheit scale, the freezing point of water is 32 degrees and the boiling point is 212 degrees.

The other scale is based on the metric system and is called **Celsius**. On the Celsius scale, the freezing point of water is 0 degrees and the boiling point is 100 degrees.

Your average body temperature is 96.4 degrees Fahrenheit or 37 degrees Celsius.

A hot day can be 80 degrees Fahrenheit which is just under 27 degrees Celsius.

A comfortable room temperature is about 20-22 Celsius.

Ice Age!

Ice ages are intervals of time – which can last tens, or even hundreds of millions, of years. Large areas of the surface of the Earth are covered with ice sheets. In between ice ages, there are equally long periods of milder climate called 'interglacials'.

Woolly mammoths survived a number of ice ages. Their thick woolly coats probably helped keep them warm!

Arctic Circle

Tropic of Cancer

Equator

Tropic of Capricorn

This map shows the spread of the ice sheet during the last ice age.

Antarctic Circle

The Earth is in an interglacial period now, but although the last ice age ended about 12,000 years ago, we can still see the polar ice sheets and mountain glaciers in Greenland, Alaska and Antarctica that are a leftover from that time.

Greenhouse effect

Greenhouses are used to grow plants, especially in winter. The glass panels let in light but keep heat from escaping, so the greenhouse heats up. Gases in the atmosphere trap energy from the Sun in the same way. Without them, heat would escape back into space, and at night-time, the temperature would drop to a freezing -40°C! Because of the way they warm our world, these gases are called greenhouse gases.

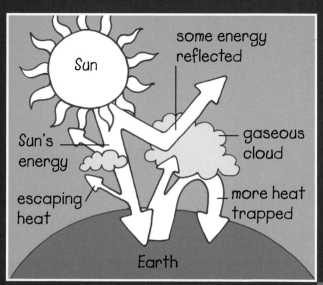

some energy reflected

Sun

Sun's energy

gaseous cloud

escaping heat

more heat trapped

Earth

Clouds

Clouds are made from tiny drops of water and ice crystals. They are so tiny and light, that they can hang in the air without dropping to the ground as rain, snow or hail. We see clouds in the sky where they form in the atmosphere. They can be very high up or close to the ground. The wind blows them in different directions and shapes.

This huge *cumulonimbus* cloud is shaped like a blacksmith's anvil.

Cloud shapes

Cirrus - these clouds form very high up in the sky. They look like wispy streaks.

Cirrostratus - these clouds look like a thin veil and usually mean that warm weather is on the way.

Cirrocumulus - these clouds are made of ice crystals and appear lower in the sky than cirrus clouds. They look like strips with rounded edges.

Altocumulus - these small rounded clouds form in groups or lines. They sometimes cause the effect of coloured rings around the moon or sun.

Altostratus - these clouds form sheets that can sometimes fill the whole sky. They can bring rain or snow.

Cumulus - these are round and fluffy and can be very tall. They often develop in warm weather.

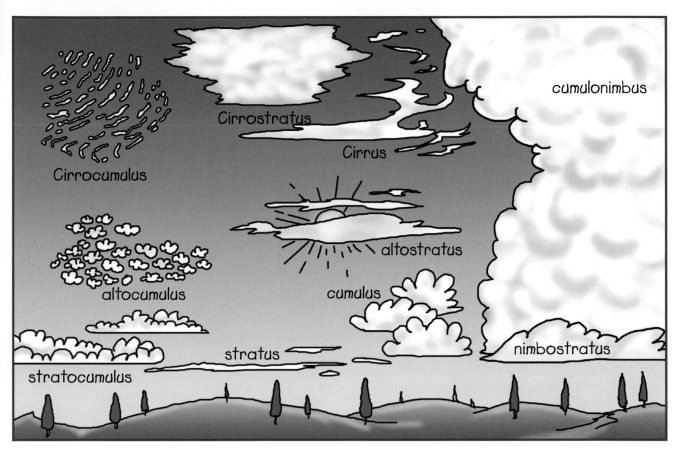

Stratocumulus - these clouds can clump together in sheets or have gaps between them. They have dark areas caused by thick rolls of cloud.

Stratus - these are low-lying clouds that form a continuous sheet. They sometimes bring drizzling rain.

Cumulonimbus - these clouds can be huge and dark grey. They bring stormy weather.

Nimbostratus - these clouds usually mean snow. They hang like a dark grey sheet across the sky.

Bang! crash!

Ancient people used to think that their gods were very angry when the sky rumbled with thunder and flashes of lightning lit the dark. Some even thought that the world was coming to an end!

Thunderstorms can certainly be very frightening. Meteorologists tell us that, at any one time, nearly 2,000 thunderstorms will be taking place around the world. These produce about 100 lightning strikes that are hitting the Earth each second. Lightning hits high buildings, chimneys, power lines and radio masts. They can be struck more than once during a single storm but aren't always damaged.

Sometimes a lightning bolt can come out of the side of the storm and strike a place several kilometres away.

Stormy weather

Thunderstorms happen when strong air currents move high up into the sky, forming huge cumulonimbus clouds that are full of rain. The rising hot air forces cold air down to the ground, forming strong winds. Powerful 'updrafts' and 'downdrafts' in the clouds also cause lightning to develop.

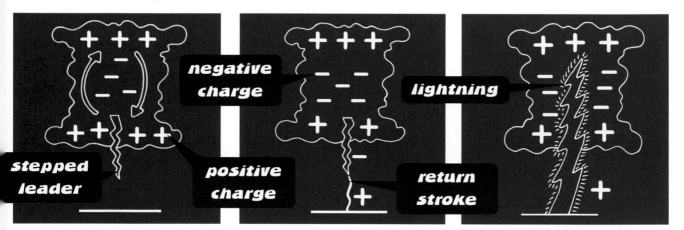

negative charge

stepped leader

positive charge

lightning

return stroke

1. The updrafts and downdrafts charge the particles in the cloud. Positive particles form at the top and bottom of the cloud, and negative particles in the middle.

A thin stroke of negative particles, known as a 'stepped leader' heads towards the ground.

2. A positive 'return stroke', rises up from the ground. This might travel up a tall object, like a chimney or telepgraph pole. It rises about 30 metres above the ground.

3. When the two strokes meet, a bright flash of electricity is made – this is the lightning we see!

The lightning travels up into the cloud where it quickly heats the surrounding air. This is what causes the thunder crash which we hear moments later.

Did you know!

The temperature inside a lightning bolt can reach 30,000 degrees C, five times hotter than the surface of the Sun!

Weather satellites

Satellites measure changes in the weather from high up above the Earth. They help forecasters to make more accurate forecasts over a longer period to come.

The Lockheed ER-2 is a special plane which can fly high above the clouds to study hurricanes. It can fly as high as 21,000 metres.

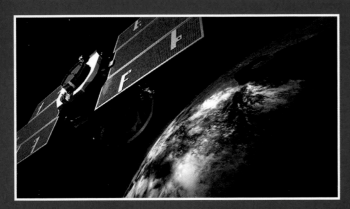

The Cloudsat satellite is being used to study clouds in ways that haven't been possible before. Scientists hope to learn a lot more about how they affect our weather.

This dramatic picture of Hurricane Rita was taken from space by the Aqua satellite on September 21st 2005. The 'eye' of the hurricane which the winds swirl around, is clear to see.

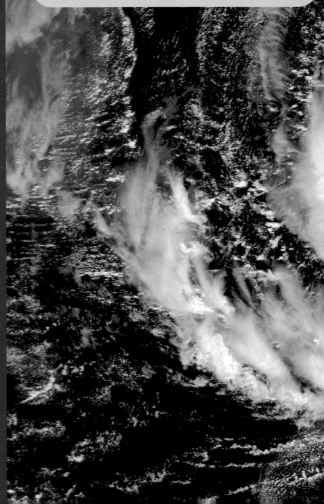

Phew! It's hot!

Heat comes from our Sun, so whenever it's shining directly onto our part of the Earth, we feel warmer. As the Earth spins around the Sun, it tilts towards different parts of the globe, so different parts enjoy lots of sunshine at different times of the year. These sunny months are called the summer season.

The Sun's heat often causes a heat haze over water.

Evaporation

Evaporation describes what happens when a liquid turns into a gas.

The sun heats up water (a liquid) in rivers or lakes, or in the ocean, and turns it into water vapour (a gas). The water vapour rises into the air as a heat haze. This is a very thin mist caused by the warm air rising off the water through the cool air above.

Hot and dry

Drought is a long period without rain. Plants and animals suffer badly during a drought and the earth dries and cracks. Deserts form in places where there are frequent droughts.

Heat wave

- While most of us enjoy the summer sun, high temperatures can be dangerous to people who aren't used to them.
- One of the biggest dangers of a heat wave is the risk of dehydration. This means our bodies lose water, and with it, important blood salts like potassium and sodium which help keep our kidneys, brain and heart working.
- Usually we sweat when we get hot, and this helps keep us cool. But on very hot days, this system can fail and our body temperature starts to climb.
- The best way to avoid heat problems is to drink water and keep in the shade.

A climatologist looks at the weather over a long period of time and often, in a specific part of the world. A country's climate depends on its position on the globe, whether it's close to the Equator or nearer to the Arctic, whether it's an island or a long way inland and far from the sea.

This map shows the different kinds of weather around the world. There are 6 main kinds. Can you find each one by matching the colours to the picture keys and descriptions?

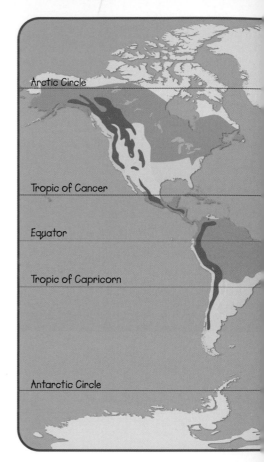

Arctic Circle

Tropic of Cancer

Equator

Tropic of Capricorn

Antarctic Circle

Tropical - hot all year. Some regions have a rainy season and a dry season.

Dry - can be very hot or cold but very little rain all year. Deserts and grasslands.

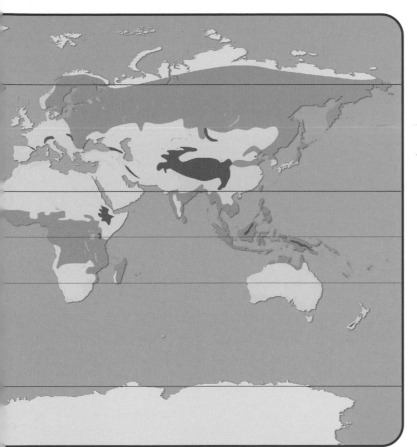

Continental - very cold winters, mild summers.

Temperate - mild or cold winters, warm or hot summers. No dry season.

Polar - very cold and dry. Covered in ice sheet most of the year. Very short summer.

Mountainous - the altitude affects the climate. High peaks are very cold.

Folklore

What did we do before weather forecasts?
Our ancestors looked for tiny signs in nature, such as changes in an animal's behaviour, to predict their local weather.

These observations have been passed down through the generations as weather folklore. While many of these tales have no scientific basis, some have been found to be surprisingly accurate and are still used in our everyday life.

1. During fine weather, insects that swallows eat are carried up high on warm currents rising from the ground.

2. Seabirds can detect shifts in atmospheric pressure that will bring bad weather.
'Seabirds, stay out from the land, we won't have good weather while you're on the sand'.

3. Bees return to their hives and are unlikely to swarm before a storm. They are probably detecting tiny changes in air pressure.

4. Fishermen say that fish 'bite' more before a rainstorm, as do small flies or midges - maybe because it's their last chance to feed before the rain.

5. If cows are lying down, you can expect rain.

6. But do you believe this one? If you keep pulling faces, one day the wind will change and you'll get stuck that way.

7. 'Red sky at night, sailors' delight. Red sky in the morning, sailors take warning'.

8. If there's a ring around the moon, it will rain in as many days as there are stars in that ring.

9. In Australia, they say: 'When the kookaburras call, the rain will fall'.

Weather Quiz

1. What type of weather does low pressure air usually bring?

_____

2. What form of weather does the Beaufort scale measure?

_____

3. What is used in a mechanical hygrometer to help measure humidity?

_____

4. What weather is shown on a weather map when the isobar lines are close together?

_____

5. At 0 degrees Celsius (32 degrees Fahrenheit) what happens to water?

6. What are interglacial periods?

_____

7. Cirrocumulus and cumulonimbus are examples of what feature of the weather?

_____

8. About how many lightning strikes are hitting the ground each second?

_____

9. What happens to a liquid when it evaporates?

_____

10. What do cows seem to be expecting when they lie down in their field?

_____

Index